The Hell of That Star

Wesleyan Poetry

ALSO BY KIM HYESOON, PUBLISHED IN ENGLISH

Phantom Pain Wings (2023)

A Drink of Red Mirror (2019)

Autobiography of Death (2018)

Poor Love Machine (2016)

Sorrowtoothpaste Mirrorcream (2014)

All the Garbage of the World, Unite! (2011)

Mommy Must Be a Foundation of Feathers (2008)

Kim
Hyesoon
김혜순

The Hell of That Star
어느 별의 지옥

Translated by
Cindy
Juyoung
Ok

Wesleyan University Press
Middletown, Connecticut

Wesleyan University Press
Middletown CT 06459
www.wesleyan.edu/wespress
어느 별의 지옥

Revised edition published in 2017 by Moonji Publishing Co., Ltd.

Designed and composed in Arnhem by Eric M. Brooks

Library of Congress Cataloging-in-Publication Data
available at catalog.loc.gov
paper · ISBN 978-08195-0218-6
ebook · ISBN 978-08195-0219-3

5 4 3 2 1

Contents

I ·

That Place 1 · 3
That Place 2 · 4
That Place 3 · 5
That Place 4 · 6
That Place 5 · 7
That Place 6 · 8
Democracy on the Village Edge · 9
The Country That Freezes as It Burns · 10
American Store on Some Day in Some Month · 11
The Tears of That Dead Man · 12
Pupil · 13
Flight · 14
Owl · 15
The Ringing of That Day · 16
A Flower That Refuses to Become Poetry · 17
Salt · 19
Big Eyes · 20
The Guy Who Went Alone · 21
Seeing Even with Patches on Both Eyes · 22
The History of Feed · 23
Map · 24
By Absence More Than Presence · 25
Back to the Past · 26

II ·

Not Even Knowing He Is Dead · 31
A Corpse Heavier Than the Whole Earth · 32
To You the Infected 2 · 33

I Should Go to the Mountains · 36
In Front of a Round Wall · 38
Harvest · 40
Every Day I Rise like Clear Glass · 41
After All the Birds Have Gone · 43
Comic Ventriloquist · 44
Madame Sun Eating Van Gogh Eating · 45

III ·

Witch Ascension · 49
Shell's Life · 50
Mom's Meal Preparation · 51
Bear with Me Please · 52
Door · 53
The Claustrophobia of a Snowy Day · 54
Glass · 55
The Hell of That Star · 56

IV ·

For the Next Instant's I · 59
Procession · 61
Big Stone · 62
Practice · 63
Person Sitting in the Front · 64
Painful Mass Games · 65
Seeing the Dead Who Came to Eat the Ancestral Offering · 66
Person Walking Backward · 67
Since There Is Nothing New Under the Sky · 68
The Way to Go · 69
Black Bird · 70
A Big Snow Is Approaching · 72
The Little Earth That Carries Me and Flows · 73
Eye · 74
A Sunday of Only Afternoon · 75

MIDSTNESS · 77
Cindy Juyoung Ok
POETRY VOICE · 83
Kim Hyesoon
NOTES · 95
ACKNOWLEDGMENTS · 97

That Place 1

THAT PLACE, that even
brightly lit shadows cannot enter,
where even with my eyes closed
inside bright sleep my skull's throbbing
I can see, bright
THAT PLACE, the world's best studio
where endless episodes strung like a rotten yellow
fish bundle are hung on spikes
THAT PLACE,
where stories and themes are made
and drop wildly like a horse's gait
onto both cheeks, both eyes, both thighs,
THAT PLACE,
outside of which lights are out black and breath held
where only I alone
like a small box with lights on
bright
THAT PLACE,

That Place 2

- *Witch burning ritual*

Even if I don't get slapped down with a whip I
get naked
Onto naked me
water falls
fog pours
dew forms

Next — the fathers come out
They come out and draw curtains outside my body
Gentle like silk! But steel curtains!
Soft like cotton! But thicker than a quilt!
Next — slap it down by the whip of the word
Next — feed it ink
My whole body fills up with ink

Finally made naked and beaten
and wearing heavy stories like clothes
onto myself I vomit out all the letters
That prophecy of the secrets
from some centuries ago
with shameful flames hanging over my whole body

That Place 3

- *Black or winter*

Trapped in THAT PLACE
As the man with the broken spine
collapsed, lips gapped in surprise
at the red apple dropped, Mother's lullaby
through F a t h e r ' s l a s h i n g s
All trapped in THAT PLACE
Cold wind was blowing and dropping the leaves off at once, pair
of round maidenhair trees facing each other with leaves shed, flesh
rotted, apple rolled along, nosebleed poured,
teeth pulled are all trapped, in THAT PLACE

THAT PLACE! Shit pit frozen into waterfall
black sealed with ten million locks!

That Place 4

▪

The woman is summoned
suddenly that day
From singing congratulations
for a friend's wedding in a field
the woman enters
through the rooms
with noodle strands each boiling
as though inside a big brain

THAT PLACE, dark lump of soy pulp
Soy pulp that, slashed with a knife, is the place of:
a father giving birth to a younger sibling
children fruited on trees
ancient times when the dragon ascended
a leopard snuck under the skirt
stars immaterially pouring—
in the side view of a bundle of soybean pulp!

The obstetrics of story and the big brother's centrality that
gives birth to plots instead of the umbilical cord and
gives birth to schemes in a curtained room instead of a placenta and
gives birth to a big-eyed big adult at corridor's end instead of a newborn
baby
Mushed soybean pulp, THAT PLACE

That Place 5

To you the beautiful
To you who rise glowingly
To you who still remain
When I cannot send my regards
what can I do
Why don't I draw a picture on the wall
and just, too, from eyeing it
In that instant interlude
when my left cheek is hit and
when my right cheek is hit
why don't I forcefully shoot off
the last remaining of my pupils
onto the wall for a moment
bending my body like a bow

That Place 6

■

Life is not only flowing about
A window unexpectedly opens in the square place
The river hits its whirl
×× endures
○○ betrays
△△ despairs
□□ dies
Still, a moment later
the river flows again
and again the whirlpool of
tens of thousands of square rooms of
THAT PLACE is built

Democracy on the Village Edge

The person who gets bigger when further
The person who stands beyond the vanishing point
and swells up like an ad balloon
The person without
substance and yet a big
mass who eats whole
missing and
sorrow and
pity and
longing
and gets bigger every day
The person an oversized figure
who presses onto me
squeezing a pack full
of my tears and my organs

When I find myself holding who is there and not there
and rolling around
The person swelling like a mountain
peak as the morning sun breaks

The Country That Freezes as It Burns

The country that freezes as it burns
fights, shoots guns, and launches nuclear warheads! As it does
the frozen over country
As events are boiling and
tangled gazes bubble and boil over
our country that threw out all the warmth it had
and became ice hell

The genius over there grasping
their burning hair and running
whose limbs are being smacked and split
already

American Store on Some Day in Some Month

Street rampant with rumors
The deeper the incident, the riper an American store vendor's shout:
It's the same underwear worn by that woman on some day in some
    month!

An alibi
An alibi for an alibi
An alibi-breaking alibi
Black market dealings
Endless linking of lips
(The sight of lips hanging from wire chattering restlessly)

The incident's dead body stuffed and hung in a secret room and
pus that bursts without even a corpse! Broken line of innards!
The corpses' heart matter swollen with water covers an American store
The guestbook of an American store on some day in some month
    instantly pours black coal tar over as soon as
the stuffed corpse is finally hung next to the signboard of the movie
    theater in an American store on some day in some month

The Tears of That Dead Man

Why eyewater comes only out of eyes
They say nosewater coming out from nose, earwater from ears
saliva from the mouth are all out of order
Why water coming out of
eyes is so easily contagious

He who let his whole body float
twenty meters deep in water
that came from his eyes and took off his whole body's grime

gathered his last breath as
he squeezed his heart and shed one drop
As he left the whole country
was swept away — bridges collapsed and trees lining
streets were uprooted
Mad pigs drifted away

Pupil

▪

The winter tree
like that: arm!
cleanly pop-torn off
spine!
snapped broken
winter tree is
but for the winter tree is
on a snowy windy winter mountain
go climb up
over there
leering seething-blue pupils
beneath the hidden
winter tree's forehead:
blue flame!
brightly turned up!

Flight

Since born into the world
I have soared only once

After A hit me and went
B jump kicked me and went and
the collapsed me C
lashed thoroughly with a whip, then
D pretended to caress me
while pounding my bruised whole body

like a strand of a flute's song I
heard
my soaring's sound

Owl

Staring contest with an owl for
an hour or two, refusing with dignity to turn its head
Pitch-dark gaze of
two black pearls
that do not tolerate even a single spot of dust

As though both my eyes are covered only with scars
as though pus is seeping from both my eyes
I clasp this cloudy darkness and
tread endlessly backward

As though sucking in ending moons of sleeping trees and sleeping beasts
as though molded of night's nucleus
a wordlessly dignified
crystal

The Ringing of That Day

My heart contained his voice
and followed me, like a bird
crying
and struck by a bird when not vigilant
That dug ate its way into both my ears
and built home deep in
While rubbing its beak

Ah Ah Ah Ah Ah Ah—

Yelling a single scream
as a layer of skin peeled off
and the flesh cooked through and through
The sounds called sounds all evaporated

Since that day wanting to cut off my ears

A Flower That Refuses to Become Poetry

Anything too cold
does not become poetry
Anything too hot
is not poetry
When soaking your feet
in boiling water
poetry does not come out
When lying in ice
with eyes wide open
poetry does not come out

That day no one wrote poetry
They only made phone calls
Picked up the receiver and secretly
blew and sent off poems
—Did you put on new clothes?
—No, just took off my old clothes
That day no one wrote poetry but
they ripped a wedding dress
to make bandages and
carried rice bowls
to use as coffins to hold each of their heads
Anything too beautiful
is not poetry
That day when they opened their mouths
and cried as though for the first time
that was not poetry

Merely
the blooming of an entire city
floating on the field of the earth —
a flower that refuses to be poetry!

Salt

On this side and that side, quietness
This side melts that side and
that side drinks this side and
the gently mixed twirling-on spring
night, this side and that side's constant osmotic pressure
Still dreams, within innards of an egg
that disappear upon shattering
    like tomorrow's morning

This side raises and stands that side up
causing its hair locks to rise and
throwing it in solitary confinement and
making salty shit tingle and
getting all sound out and
spilling beans of unrest into the bloodstream at
high noon, sleepless spring
water, black roots stretched under two feet
with two fingers shoved into two eyes
to not melt
to not doze and meld in
afternoon, opium drowned in boiling water
No no please — and then
peeing salty water cascade

Big Eyes

▪

As though unraveling
rolls of cotton cloth—
unravel the knots in your joints and
lie your whole body down
to unravel it infinitely and
in your chest's valley
let birds rest—
from both shoulders let sprout pine trees
chestnut trees and cypress trees—
stretch as river water on your face
thuds! let it burst and flow
and even try to suddenly birth
a single sweetfish—
become also the big eye that
gazes at that sweetfish laying eggs—
let Pacific Ocean hurl
under your toes and
the tombs covering
bodies inside pop up and out
to throw far
fat scarecrows
rising from under the flesh
—high in the air
as high as the sun
lift up
your aching heart
as it flutters open
above the mass of earth

The Guy Who Went Alone

When spring comes again one you will become seven
and thirty will be born of seven
Born in both Gyeongsang-do and Jeolla-do at the same time
Just as straw bales pile into all the internal organs
thousands of Gildongs appear at the same time daily
blooming perennially in that way
So the white, cold
breathless
scissors, in the paralysis of night
become the scissor ghosts that carelessly grip
the tails we hold and hide in our weary sleep and cut
You, the guy who went and died alone

Seeing Even with Patches on Both Eyes

■

Like giving away all my wealth
to buy a single black pearl
I must sell my whole body
to buy one eye

The saving eye
that sees once then
never forgets
The eye that does not rot even when buried
I must buy the black pupil that doesn't burn

The eye that stares at me intently
with open eyes
even with patches on both eyes
If I resolutely cut my life off
my neck would not be cut off but
first in front of me the world would be
cut off resolutely and
then, like yeast, swollen
pupils
A life only of pupils

The History of Feed

▪ *A record of four thousand years of history*

The rail thin woman devours a fat man / She devours him cleanly with not a single toenail leftover / After eating, she keeps looking around to eat again / The more she eats, the skinnier the skinny woman gets / The stick thin woman devours all the fat men and fat women / So fat men and fat women that are eaten become the blood and flesh of the stick thin woman / Hunger leads to hungry blood and hungry flesh that call for hunger / The stick thin hungry woman tries to eat again even after eating everything / Her eyes get bigger and her teeth get sharper / Her hunger gets worse, and the woman can't withstand it, so she cuts up the ground and eats it / Then she cuts off her breasts and eats them and cuts up the rest of her body and eats that too / She also dislodges her pupils and eats them and crunches and munches on her skeleton and eats that / Well, before long now, it is the Pacific Ocean hurtling all at once toward the rail thin woman's maw that you shall see

Map

Under the blue sky
clouds in full bloom

With one ear in each hand
I grab and pull
(wait for the brief tearing sound)

Clouds floating by
dividing up the sky among themselves

open my heart's door and
put your wrists in
Your fists pounding the sky
Electric static
rain shower, free fall

A few drops of acetic acid from blue sky to torn clouds
American clouds under that sky
Asian clouds and South Korean clouds!

By Absence More Than Presence

Love is by absence
Peace is by absence
Freedom is by absence

Freedom is beyond presence

He by absence screams
He by absence is pulled long
He by absence becomes sick

And so I also by absence
because of absence
turn away
the desperately try to stay me

Back to the Past

■

She's walking here
She's loosening her hair and untying her hanbok ribbons
and walking here
When everyone is flowing along,
when they're waving their fins
as they go,
the woman
who returns alone to
lightly sprinkle salt

is running here
She's holding up her skirt's edge and
dancing while coming
When all is flowing along
with shoulders interlocked
the woman
who returns alone to
slap someone's cheeks
and pour vomit on their head

is flying here
With no eyelids and
no lips,
the woman who is only a hole
lays eggs in a rock's crack and
when all is flowing once more
sticks out a dagger

to head against the tide
toward a past life and
once a month smells of blood
the woman

Not Even Knowing He Is Dead

Not even knowing he is dead he
gets up in a hurry
Over his hollow-emptied chest
he gently ties a necktie and
on his crisp-dried hair
he applies oil and
into the intestines from which maggots crawl
he pours milk and
over his dead feet-leather
he puts on leather shoes and
through a tombstone-lined street
he dashes like wind

Not even knowing he is dead he
comes back dusting himself off
When he lays a blanket
next to a dead woman's coffin
and bends over
his hairs pour and pile
and cold teeth pour into his mouth
Then wrinkled skin
falls around his feet and
not even knowing he is dead he
dies again as he
smacks out wonderful
words to be engraved on his tombstone tomorrow and
pulls the coffin lid up himself

A Corpse Heavier Than the Whole Earth

■

They rush in to invade when I die
The foods I ate my whole life
The words I spit my whole life
The shits I laid my whole life
The waters I drank my whole life
all raid rushing in
and into my body they return
Once returned
they amass systematically
from my bowels to my throat
So eventually I
hold and carry
the whole earth in my body
heavier than that rock and
slip deep into the after life

To You the Infected 2

When fever blooms like a flower in my armpit
and my pulse rings like thunder on my wrists

When doctors who guide life away come in
and the mural of a lifetime is abruptly fading away

Last shot!
Gold-colored breath that blooms for 10 seconds! Loud will and testament

> —Do I present to you the hell:
> drink golden water and
> coat your body in golden paint, be stiff

Suddenly you open the door
put both your feet up
on the bed from which I departed
wearing oxygen masks
You the next generation starting
to get sick, you the contagious ones

One time within death
One time within life
While dipping in and taking out
While taking out and dipping in

A rotten decayed hope, that if one bite
of it is thrown, comes breaking in
again quickly through the mouth, one bite
fed, when taken away

and vomiting, again, while feeding
while hitting
while saliva, spitting
while soothing
while medicine, giving

When imposing life into it and taking it out
taking it out. Again.
While injecting

> —Come on, why not try
> Even if you run away to inside
> your mind I know
> the beginning of the haze
> Why not
> put out the culprit of representation

But in the deep night
when it is not when
they are asleep
terror arrives on horseback
The IV needle flees
and only then the blood
in my temple bursts
and the terror and I
that have become one body
burst from my bare body
When I'm sinking
into gold-lit darkness
my eyes do not avert from
those who have already left
waiting for me
with red carpet laid

and the incense stick reserved
for my funeral burning

One person moos and goes and
gets stuck in the soil
One person oinks
and goes and gets stuck in the soil

A wagon loaded full
of a lifetime leaves first
and a world where only shadows are left
in unison! Open the golden gate
and come in!

I Should Go to the Mountains

■

I should go to the mountains
Should cook white rice for the family that remains,
to eat until full and then sing,
light a bright fire in the fireplace,
bend my back,
wrap a rope around my head,
cross shallow mountains,
cross deep mountains,
and go to the mountains

Midnight steadily loosens seeping into the ground and
deep mountains loosen their belts and swell up
Night when mountain and night ferment like cold porridge
the old days of my life are
coughcoughing
Night spitting
c · r · o · w · c · r · o · w
I should go to the mountains
I should go alone

I should go to the mountains
To black rice and black death and black hunger and black cold
and black pain
I give it all away and
under a black soul
heavier than a rock
I should lay my body down
and watch my disappearing

pupils sparkle
for the last time
I should go on foot
to go and starve to death

In Front of a Round Wall

If I post a letter
it returns back
If I send love
circling the earth round
my beloved wrists
come back soon and
shatter under my feet

If I fly a bird
the bird flies away
and embeds into me and
if I tip a lifetime over
to leak it away
riverwater goes
and returns again and
if I spread my limbs out
to send them to the sky
the sky bends back returning
to land horizon and water horizon and

in this way
on the last day
in front of a wailing round wall
I to you
throw curses
Yes this one
Hurry out now

and take your poison!
And then
quickly I hold the poison bowl
and drink it away

Harvest

The field that lies down
saying it's finished
The autumn that gives out its neck
saying it's been fought

That which rolls around wrestling with heat
saying I won't lose
That which strangles and screams screams
in a pitch-dark storm
saying I won't cry

This chest sinking
by straw-wrapped branches in kindling ashes
saying it's finished

Every Day I Rise like Clear Glass

You wouldn't know
That every night I
quietly lay myself down and
go to you

You also wouldn't know this
That every night you
leave yourself
to come meet me

That the two of us hold hands and
cross the Jordan River
wearing petals on our naked bodies and
blowing sparks
from our mouths while
flying with the earth hanging from our ankles
You really wouldn't know

That in deep night the two of us
float like clear glass,
drink sky, swallow moon,
and without even a shadow
embrace

And you wouldn't know this either
That after the night passes
I return again
without a sound
and lie back down

That I turn off the lights
and bury flower stems
deep in the ground
And that it is my spirit
I conceal

After All the Birds Have Gone

The tough after all
we still remain
and just in gathering it is lovingly
even while building each other's tombs
while patting each other's backs

But when each bird turns around
their arms flung! open
embracing tightly what
they do not even recognize as their grave
and they hug and hold harder and harder
stretching four limbs out over the laid sleeping mat and blanket
saying I love you I love you even in their sleep
In this world from which crying birds have disappeared
only I am left

Comic Ventriloquist

Wearing a black hat and
carrying a black cane and
fluttering the tail of a black tuxedo
as though conducting a funeral

Covering and covering myself
I pull down my cuffs but

like a doll popping suddenly out the stomach
there is a time for curse
words to be spat like seeds

If I shut the doll's mouth
my mouth is blocked and
there is a time when
like held-back laughter
death bursts from stomach without warning

When I take off my black gloves and put on my black hat and turn to go—
such is an end without an end

Madame Sun Eating Van Gogh Eating

Boiling field porridge
of barley field road cut into slices
for rust-colored stew
splashed with sunflower seeds and
mixed by rice paddle's whirwhirring—
Van Gogh's meal preparation

His breaking spinal fluid puhlpulsing
like a cauldron as time sifts,
a more violently boiling whirlpool
infinite bursting of his skull
that makes the hands holding field porridge
with a paddle tremble wildly
Van Gogh's head of a lid open in
the age of boiling noodles
Madame Sun's meal preparation

III

Witch Ascension

If I open the window would morning sky unfold there
If I go a bit further from there might I see the sea

There must be dirt under the window and grass beetles that lounge
and there I must be on the grass
Would I close my eyes
My head would be shattered I bet
My pelvis must also have shattered
How high a place would it be that
they would sweep me up and away again
To carry then throw me in a shed
They would

Lying alone in a cell
suspended in the air
I rot

Shell's Life

▪

You a stuffing genius who
instantly take out intestines
throw out hot blood
leak brain fluid out
dry flesh and bones
then fill the body with bright cotton
that does not even show a shadow

I see you and smile involuntarily
because of the toilet paper wad in your lips
I see you and the inside of my mind is bright
I see you and take off my clothes
because your insides are bright

I see you and my face reddens
because you paint it

You a stuffing genius with
the ends of your nerves
dangling off ends of my nerves
the end of your brush hanging
from the end of my veins

The long road I walked rattlingly
in the way you led
I extended my arms in the way you lead,
upper lip lower lip that fluttered on
the long, long road

Mom's Meal Preparation

It is said it was after father's bomb exploded

They were being baked
Fat splattered and rose and
sparks splattered and
skin burned into
like in a microwave
On one side with skin hanging rag-like from its skeleton
some stood inside fire
Others were mashed like tomatoes
There was also being pressed against a huge stone
until smashed like tofu
As their stomachs pop-pop exploded
there was a foul stench
Not knowing who was coming to eat them
the whole field
was painted in tears as
they were being fried

Mother swallowed her tears as she prepared the meal

Bear with Me Please

I will plop into my body
a well bucket and draw water
With that water I'll wash the rice
I'll serve a delicious dinner

I'll loosen flesh and mix blood
to toss into the chewy japchae too
As the deep mountain that can no longer bear it bursts spring water
I'll receive welling tears and
add on a glass of mountain water
With a blooming breath
I will decorate for you
the warmth of the dinner table

So bear with me please
Please don't get angry that
inside the rice bowl are an unshatterable
few stones
Even if you think
that stone is my true will
I beg you, bear it generously and just swallow please

Door

Toward that dark night
Toward the corpses' waiting
Toward an infinitely deep down well
In front of children crying
without even tears
In front of women in mourning clothes
In front of coffin bearers sprinkling stones
The door of the prison closes and opens
The door of death closes and opens
The soft flesh making up the door of your lips
even without knocking
closes and
again
opens

The Claustrophobia of a Snowy Day

When I shout far
the sound returns
like a heavy stone in my chest
Inside my chest there is also
a mountain and there is
an ocean and there is a road
On the road in the ocean in that mountain
stones
are scattered
Thousands of hundreds of millions are
scattered away
Even when I shout far
no matter to whom
it seems no one can hear me
When I sing on a snowy day
stones pour out
from my eyes, ears, and mouth
Stones rain down
both inside and outside and
no one can see the sun

Glass

On me
you all leave no handprints
On me
you do not stain
It's just
as if only all your shadows slipped
On me
you cannot even unload your weight
Neither body temperature
nor whip reaches
To me
even your sweet voice does not reach
There are no hot tears either
But I
know I will shatter at once
In morning sunlight
with ten million strands
twinkling
I know I will cut out all your eyeballs
and fly away in an instant

The Hell of That Star

The tomb is here
as two mounds hanging from the chest
The place below which people of centuries ago are still
buried and breathing
As moon rises and sets over the sea
under two tombs
dead ones gather and
the deep body of woman that
raises and pulls the moon
spreading out the vast sea
is a palace of another world
The place where darkness of centuries ago is still
trapped and bleeding
but that stretches
when crescent moon rises
The place where snakes kiss snakes and
green grass tree vines are revived
and razed thousands of times over
The hell of that star is here

IV.

For the Next Instant's I

When I hold a cigarette in my left hand and
light a lighter with my right hand
the diapered infant I has on a white
collar, the schoolgirl I wears high heels,
and the stumbling I tonight,
the I that was swearing and drinking with you, the I from just
now, the I that is everyone is who
holds a cigarette in my left hand and
lights a lighter with my right hand

After the next instant when I let out smoke from my two nostrils
many nostrils will send off
two strands of white smoke

When I lace the wine glass between my fingers again
and pour alcohol into my mouth
it's dozens of fingers interlacing wine glasses and
dozens of open mouths drinking while
among even dozens of hearts
in the loudest voice the I that is about to change the diaper of the baby of
    the diapered infant I and the next instant's I—

Then after the next instant you slap my cheeks! To alert me and as I stand
I, I—I—I—I—I
even among them the over-thirty woman I is the very last to stand
sounding dozens of waves
straightening the one-year-old fingers like a fern
two, three, four year olds
straightening of the fingers the finger with also a ring

pointing at me, the dozens of women
in a shrieking voice
I said I am I!
I'm saying don't touch me!

Procession

Like an old large bookshelf is page by page
torn down
Like a single mulberry tree pitter-patters
dropping mulberry leaves
Like a mural buried by time, dusting off
little by little
Past lives go walking on

When I drink a sip of water
a past life's woman dies in the shade of a mulberry tree
When I drink a sip of alcohol
this world's me under one layer of soil today and now

Like an old large bookshelf is torn down and
one mural fully revealed
a drunk me gazes at the me in the drawing
with indifference

When that past life's woman dies
holding a peach close in
her hands like a young daughter
I'll carry an empty sack saying
It's war, it's war
and under an old large bookshelf
again go to hide

Big Stone

▪

This damn stone that, if I close my eyes,
appears like a boss on a desk's
very center! This stone that, if I—pop—kick it,
sits on my ankle!
The disgusting bastard! I put it on top of my neck and precariously
walk   When it sleeps: on a pillow like a boss

stone · heavy stone · big stone · dolmen stone ·
(with effort) Take · this · stone · and · throw · it · up!
Far dist   ant!
(as my face gradually reddens) Throw · it · like · a · discus · thrower!

Like my tombstone above me!
There is a stone that cannot be hugged closely or trampled over
or chewed and swallowed
That stays on my eye like a stye but
presses me down more than an island: big
stone!

Practice

Each day it comes and
wakes us up and
orders us to practice
There is a way to die like this
Like this, to get up and stretch out
Eat to fill and explode the stomach like this
Go out of breath from delight heehee like this
In hopeless conversations
shared words are cut off just as
the pulse is lost like this
There is too a way to die like this
Each day it comes and
puts us to sleep and
orders us to practice again
While hiding a heart so indecent
it mumbles words of blessing

Person Sitting in the Front

■

He was in the midst of riding the train
His death awaited at
the train's last stop
He was even sitting
in the train's aisle
He and the train were both going toward death

He took off his hat
He took off his shoes
He took off his coat
As though the thought occurred, he took off his watch
A moment later he started to vomit
his unraveling skull from his nostrils
and mouth onto the floor

The final stop is soon
It is not soon yet but
soon will come soon and as
soon
as tomorrow morning
in front of him and me sitting face to face like this
as if empty
Soon
He is
Yes, now — soon

Painful Mass Games

The dead singer
circles the earth and
still does not stop their song
Turning like a vinyl record
of some rowing song
or like a revolving stage
circling

On stage
the dancers jump up
like potatoes sticking out of the ground
or molding faces out of clay
storming then return to the ground
to seep and
stand up again and lie down again
These mass games
run on eternally

So still I follow the beat of your song
appearing then leaving and
disappearing again while
switching partners and
switching faces and
wondering if it is a dream or life, a lover or guest,
while welcomingly delighting and
not missing a step
until I let go of your wrist

Seeing the Dead Who Came to Eat the Ancestral Offering

▪

Me, I see
I can't see and then I see
Me, I see only what is invisible
Me, I don't see what is visible
I see and then I can't see

If I close my eyes, myself now buried under
sand is what I see so I know I'm in trouble
If I lie in the bathtub hehe
in the coffin a wide-eyed
me younger than me is what I see
I see the time I was talking to my mother's heart
so I'm in trouble, a huge disaster, trouble that has burst
I see the dead eating the ancestral offering
They rush here running
painted entirely in blood and once again die
As I see them fall over,
I'm in big trouble, a serious disaster
Dead thud on top of my rice bowl
thumping and falling over, I'm in trouble

Person Walking Backward

Inside the head there lives a lonely dog
that is drooling spit
digging through a mountain pile of garbage
opening and closing an empty house's windows
overturning footprints in the sand
and going into the fog

When you're walking poundingly today
with a clock hung on your heart
When you're hanging the hour and second hands from your legs today
and rowing this way and that
When the road you have walked today
is quickly followed and erased by someone
When inside your head a dog
wags his tail and
stands with its back to you
digging through the garbage pile
while indifferently watching
a bird falling to death

Since There Is Nothing New Under the Sky

Even reading a book, it's all been said and heard
Even reading poetry, it's been heard some other time
——Then I love you
…… Words I've long heard
——I don't like you
…… Words I've heard oh so many times
——Congrats! Your death
…… Always heard of and lived it
——This is really fucking
…… Even laughably
——You're really going to be like this?
…… Words forgotten as soon as you turn around
——Two thousand years(thunder!) dead(lightning!) he(clap!) is he(bolt!) re
resurr(thunder again!)ected (thunder again again)! He! Has! Come!
…… I told you not to believe it

Whatever I heard yesterday
I will spout again tomorrow and
what I said tomorrow you will hear again yesterday
but
here
while tilting
Mommy I am hungry
Right! First time hearing that

The Way to Go

My hair is a burning charcoal lump
but my feet are ice

When I lie down the whole room is in flames
When I stand up the whole room is an ice warehouse
Mom, mom come here and look at this,
a young daughter beckons while
a black rat digs through a burning head
and waits in front of the fontanelle
The continuously visible road
was this far away

I go without going, I go while washing my feet with my hair
Even if I don't leave I leave organically
He is holding a baton waiting
Even if I walk backward I go straight
I go even if I hide in the dirt
Amid black trees, forest stars, sky, an owl opens its eyes
and goes without running
The blue light was on, soon the blue light turns on

When I lie down fire catches
and says to go
and if I run my legs break
Even if my body goes the mouse in my body doesn't go and
even if I don't go I go

Black Bird

Above each head
there lives a bird
Nested on top of the brain
laying eggs
it lives indifferently

Rolled up feathers
dried in the sun and
even while brushing
are worshipping

Quickly put both hands
on the crown of your head
Black bird flapping feathers

Keep the beak upright
to eat the eyeballs
Open the wings then
cover the ears and

look out now
You will see me
barely holding my neck
lifting my head's crown
and shaking while
swinging my legs
Sometimes picking my earflaps
Sometimes opening and closing my eyelids
docilely

And touch at least my lips
Mhm I couldn't hear
Mhm I said I couldn't see
That, I'll just keep saying that

A Big Snow Is Approaching

Mountain of water!
Silver mountain that
on foul weather days
returns and stands tall,
mountain risen by the liquid skeleton of ghosts
that walks toward me!

The vigorously approaching
grand march of tears of remorse
knocking my throat
until my breath chokes!
Mountain of water opening its big eyes full of tears
wrapping me in silver starting with my head
running
flooding, by any means unstoppable
big
mountain!

—Oh oh oh! Wait a minute!
I will flow first and
in front of me, mountain of water

The Little Earth That Carries Me and Flows

Though sometimes we may say
it's not scary as we walk
Though sometimes we may say we've subtly
put our fists up through walls
Though sometimes we may say we've climbed
the wall and flown recklessly
over lake, mountains, and sea
Though sometimes we may say we've strayed from narrow
paths and roamed across pathless mountains alone

Earth the size of my soles is always beneath my feet
Sky the size of my palms rests above my head
They carry and flow me along
like a small raft sliding down the river

Eye

Just look at that
A plane or so
crashing into the snow
isn't anything, I told you
A volcano could explode
and I do not even blink
an eye at all

Eyes that don't burn even looking at fire
Eyes that don't overflow even while looking
The greedy ghost of those scooped big eyes
that can never be satisfied
That black stomach pocket connected to a black hole

Appalling eyes that don't overflow
even if opened wide in water,
disgusting
When is it you'll come down and walk around
Or not just look but open your eyes

A Sunday of Only Afternoon

Blue sky
looked at by falling rain

White paper
gazed on by ruined drawing

Buried person
stared at by black crow

Morning
that looks back on afternoon waking

Daughter's springlike morning song
listened to as the breath cuts off

Midstness

▪ *Cindy Juyoung Ok*

Kim Hyesoon's poetics is one of ghosts and deaths, of absences and existential contingencies. Writing over almost fifty years in ways estranged, singular, and taut, her attentions have wound comprehensively but remain painfully particular. She was born two years into the Korean ceasefire that holds today and came of age amid state censorship and murder, turning to poetry that concerns the death of words, self, and people, which grief has surveilled and fractured across languages. Korea's placement in the world order changes over Kim's books, the violence of a military regime in this collection, which has turned into the violence of a neoliberal power in other recent collections. The mode of domination and its images are different, the inhumanity constant. Death and nationalism intersect corporeally, cataloging rot, burning, and burial, seemingly from their interiors, their holes.

The Hell of That Star considers ends of all kinds from the position of their middles, the innards of the logical and sometimes destructive extremes of language or knowledge or desire. In poems against and from dictatorships that defined the 1970s and 1980s in Seoul, where Kim lived, death is not a sudden, momentary threat but a sustained and ongoing reality to recognize and accommodate, much like life. Death is not opposed to living, is instead the condition for its confirmation. Kim's poems declare that accumulating consumption and perception are rarely gratifying and that even mortality has its own consciousness. Each appears whole, as though out of the mist and into the midst—of decay, domestication, threat, and aloneness. The poet offers an invitation to stay within cyclical, incidental death, where a word is actor, enactment, and acted upon. The book stretches with unusual gestures and defies with increasingly deeper designs; it echoes where it cannot utter and lives where it has already died.

When Kim first gave me her blessing to translate this book, she asked me to convey the voice of the 소녀, the girl. This voice cries out from under the social and economic turmoil of the US-backed Korean dictatorship and the sustained, deadly resistance against it. The title poem "The Hell of That Star" takes place in graves beneath two mounds, invoking the military practice of mutilating and removing young protestors' breasts in Gwangju as well as Phong Nhị. So much is written and known about how war affects girls and women in towers of empire, but this book's locus is those whose bodies they take as collateral. With intense observance and mourning awareness, the young voice details rather than narrates experience.

To write of being in the midst or middle of something, in Korean using 중에 often creates a progressive tense: I am in the midst of writing, you are in the midst of reading, we are in the midst of dying. Indicating the in-between and the among, gerunds are well used by poets and their ghosts, by ghosts and their poets. Kim identifies what she calls a middle space, or middle ground—중간지대—where poetry houses the voice between air's possibility and the ground's actuality.

The living dead in this volume not only breathe; they mumble and sing, vomit and scream. They get dressed and wonder, run and fall, also die (again). These poems disturb the concept of the afterlife by figuring an afterdeath—of the routines and languages and bowels of corpses. They are compositions of decomposition. The dispatches from the dead are perpetually in the midst of some process or action—sitting on train floors, introducing hell to the next patient, gathering with one another.

The six poems that open the book were from a series of seven the author wrote shortly after being slapped seven times by a government official during a highly censored period when she was an editor. The specter of that seventh poem, a poem of curses not included, seems also indicative of the young voice, a sincere midstness of despair untranslatable and unredeemable. The person at the publishing house whose information she was safeguarding was a literary translator, one deemed subversive.

■

Translation from Korean to English is an imperial realm; several systems have been invented for the military, tourism, and other so-called official purposes of various nation-states. These alphabets map and orient by assuming language to be a controlling totality. Transliterations, transcriptions, and translations are then deemed correct based on their closeness to these equivalences chosen by scholars and government officials sharing a desire to capture and homogenize.

Like military translation, literary translation is often discussed as a problem to be solved, counted, and assessed in terms of loss, use, exchange, or sacrifice. Many of the rules of language we internalize are, after all, rules of war. They may center production and results; proof and faith; arithmetic and capital. Translation is a means of solidarity but also of assimilation. Under its rules, veneers of methodology may be mistaken for accuracy. Impulses to create and uphold internal canons, even individual canons, risk situating literature as static, refusing to imagine that the direction of action, the domain of diction, or sound's symbolisms are all relative and changing. Those of us born into translation grow up to be borne by it.

Whereas writing a poem begins and ends, translating a poem stays in midsts. I begin with existing text instead of a ruled blank page and make a series of decisions likelier to be conscious. Those decisions do not cease when a poem has been translated and edited then published; each time I read a poem I have translated, another version (or seven) may occur to me. I marvel, for example, at the flexibility and relativity of tense in Kim's poems, which occur multiply across conventional partitions of past, present, or future. Hers is a poetry of present aftermath—of the annihilation absolute but not completed, of the past yet also ongoing. What is left as glass shatters at once, bridges have collapsed synchronously, or sky will arch back to ground? She presents a conception of time close to memory and experience: elliptical, evolving, severe, even sunken. Such midstness. I wrote and rewrote several translations into many tenses, shapes, and sounds as their boundaries relaxed, each true in their way, and in a few instances appearing with a new verb tense, including those not technically existent in Korean. Confronted by constant potential mortalities, troubling essentialisms of tense, repetition, or divisions of time can become momentarily fragile and irrelevant. A poem can draw breath in such a moment.

The niceties that typically begin and end Korean emails became intimacies in my back-and-forths with the author as I translated this book. We remarked on the state of various horrors: the international policing complex, the difficulty of sustained bodily pain with aging, the pandemic and its conditions, my grandmother's death from the virus in complete isolation in Seoul, or mass death by crowd crush in Itaewon. With marked perception of and commitment to the afterdeath of words, Kim's personal notes were often funny and always generous as we encountered one another's work in the midst of losses, uprising, and time. When I wondered about permission to include some lingual play or to reorient a line break, she eluded the structure of my questions and their assumption of authority, despite "authority" containing, in English, the author. She urged me not to think of her work as a historical document centering fact and reminded me that poetry, poetic voice, is most important. The voice of the 소녀, the girl.

▪

Despite being directly created and maintained by the US, this authoritarian period in Korean history is contextually bare in English language poetry and spare even in Korean literature due to the brutal government suppression of art. As an editor, Kim delivered manuscripts redacted by officials' hands to her writers, and her own writing tensed and shrank against these cruel limits, struggling to live in the midst of the coal used to tar pages. State censorship threatens not only a society's art, but also its artists—the inspectors within who begin to ration language and thought.

Against those excisions, Kim's poems sometimes refuse to make *sense*, creating in the wake of logic's myth an original syntax and estranged diction. In the new material of her language, "I" is a site where the personal and political meet to escape containment, domestication, and emptiness. Her words invoke and abandon structures of masculinity and capitalism, pointing to the power of narrative to both oppress and liberate. Unable to name those names, her speaker alternates blithe confidence and trembling terror—each masking a communal grief, each marking exiles of mind and body. The poetic forms lean toward the structure of a question, not an answer.

Translation likewise does not have to lay claim—can instead add, free, and assemble. Claiming, as a speech act, is legal, financial, and colonial: the language of conquest necessitates the conquest of language. An anti-nationalist translation may require the refusal of translation's law and order, given Korean translation's long use by the West for the domination of the country, now a dominator that funds and uses translation for soft power. The value of translating books is often appraised by the access and connection it brings to readers, but the calculation risks serving a depoliticized cultural reign. Kim's words on and off the page divest from, have no interest in, such reign, which may entail rhetorical definitiveness or lingual ownership. Such lores of language and their designated constructions can subjugate, whereas her writing refuses devotion to language or country, stanzas and whole poems doubting the unit of the sentence with varied styles and shifting practices.

Choosing to struggle with linguistic elements is sometimes a translator's most direct counter to the priorities of dominion. How to preserve a repeating sound or carry an amusing idiom or homonym? To what end is the syllable count shared or an image remade? Just as Kim writes not about death but from death, from within its very gaps, translation can be conceived of and practiced as a generative art of perforations, recognizing that all texts are mediated and each reader on different and intersecting axes. Negotiations with source texts and collaborations with authors are determined by time and place, by material and experience. In *The Hell of That Star*, no abandoned body disintegrates quickly; a translation of poetry is a kind of living corpse, an afterdeath of language. The translator lives out this death.

South Korea, 대한민국, has a more frequent colloquial term, 우리나라, which appears in these pages (an analogous term is also used in North Korea). It is made up of "our" and "country," but to translate it as such could convey a nationalism that it does not hold, especially because in Korean, particularly in certain regions and contexts, "our" is used in place of "my," as in "our house" and "our wife." It is the sort of plural world from which Kim writes, of 의태어 and 의성어 (mimetic words and onomatopoeic words), of homonyms and transegmental drift.

In working so closely with the hells and stars in this collection, translation became an act alive amid existing words and texts; from this midst, I could reimagine the space of rupture as full, as among. To translate midstness itself is to translate not only sentences but connotations, custom, and momentum—not just words but relationships between the words, between their parts of speech, accepting what cannot be translated. It discards the assumption that equivalence is realizable and wanders away from the central authority of a text or translator. Sawako Nakayasu notes that the "errant translator," willing to fail codes and betray theories, "may translate the beautiful, but they also translate the vomit." *The Hell of That Star* honors me with the role of translating vomit and other beautiful horrors: shit, maggots, and nothingness. Translating midstness leverages invention and terror, of frustration and care. Toward an ambition to unsettle and to create, not to obey or to copy.

The volume acknowledges the collective national horror of a specific era, but pivots on the utterances, feelings, and concerns of one woman, which is poetry's profound possibility. I have been lucky to translate this collection, and luckier to realize that Kim Hyesoon's commitment to living reality, not explaining it, aligns with her poems' center in every language: liberatory even when mournful. My mind has been revised by her trust in me as a translator, in poetry as a world, and in writing across languages, beyond in-betweenness, toward midstness. A reader, too, can be changed by Kim's confidence in the reader of her poems. I translate these gaps between and within words, the ghost of the poet, and of the translator, each poem a collaboration across years, ocean, and honor.

Poetry Voice

▪ *Kim Hyesoon*

When I first started working at a publishing house, the dictatorial Yushin regime was seemingly reaching its late stages.

At the time the state censored all newspapers, books, and magazines that were to be printed and distributed. In those days books were made by letterpress printing: each letter was individually composed by type setters and pickers, then corrected by me in the editorial department. Once they were corrected again and again, proofs were copied and bound in book form and taken to City Hall, where soldiers in military uniforms sat—gathered as though in a publisher's office—and censored texts by poets, novelists, and other writers. Before returning them, they painted the letters or pages that they would not allow to be published with black coal tar. They reigned as the publishing house over all publishing houses, the printing press above all printing presses, holding red felt-tipped pens and black coal tar instead of type.

It was impossible to know why a given stretch of text was erased. As with the songs banned in our country, those reasons were known only to the people censoring, who produced excuses for erasing letters, excuses that daily became more varied and numerous than sentences themselves could be produced in books. Common excuses were that a text was not wholesome; caricatured soldiers; included the word *freedom*; had an unacceptable author or translator; used some impermissible reference; violated societal morals; was an act of treason; was written at night instead of the author sleeping; would have a bad influence on children; was nauseating; grumbled of failures; showcased an unlikeable character; and so on.

Though I never cried when I retrieved a censored book, I did cry when I had to meet with the authors after to explain the circumstances of their books' tarring. When I visited R, an economist who was about to publish his life's last work, I had to declare, to his death bed, the death of the book before the death of the author. His wife spoke for him, saying he had hoped to see the book published before he died. From bed the economist simply cried, wordless. Tears flowed from inside his long, creased glasses toward the backs of his ears.

This experience as an editor atrophied my poetry writing — reducing the word count of my poems, stiffening their rhythm, modulating my voice — and turned my poetry into ruins of themselves. Within my poems, I killed my direct experience. The experience of being deprived of words was the experience of my tongue dying first, before my own death. It was the experience of death permeating from my tongue to my whole body. The moment I spoke, I would be killed, but the censors also killed me even by not letting me — us — speak.

▪

Once when I was the editor of a play to be published in conjunction with its theater run, they painted everything from title to contents into a mass of coal tar. The title was *Doghorn* (an expression like "dogshit"), and I can still vividly hear the young soldier's voice saying, "But dogs don't have horns, do they?" They erased the play title, claiming dogs don't have horns so such a title insults art. Eventually, only the names of the author and the publisher were left alone and all contents of the book were redacted like charred remains.

I went to the author's office holding that charcoal-like book with both my hands. He was then working at an office for the popular movement where several other employees had been imprisoned for forming a secret circle toward building a socialist state. When I handed the author the lump of charcoal his manuscript had disappeared into, he was calm. Still, his face and body seemed to sharpen into the blade of a knife. A fierce blue ambiance clouded around the author. I thought, this person must pass through this era and this country with that blade-like face, that look in his eyes and body. Since he couldn't publish the book, he suggested I come and see the play's performance. Every line of the play has been cut out, but to come see the performance — I wondered to myself — what does he mean by performance, is it a secret underground performance? But he told me to come to the famous Cecil Theater near City Hall. The writer had prepared my seat, front row center of the theater, and was waiting.

I watched the performance. Throughout the entire play, there was no voice. Every line of dialogue had been erased. There was only the movement of the actors, and unlike pantomime, their movement did not represent or exaggerate anything. The edit to the play was solely that none of the actors made a sound, however long they stood on stage. No one in the audience could know how the actors were internally reciting the lines they had memorized over months on that stage.

A few times during the performance, sounds poured out like terrifying screams. It sounded like a noise heard during a police station interrogation, bursting out of nowhere from the next room. Then, immediately after, there was the sound of mumbled screams being chewed and swallowed inside the mouth. The actors did not open their mouths, but the time they spent memorizing their lines was transformed into moans that, unable to be withstood, exploded. There must have been a director's instruction to the actors to "Only gesture!" but there were moments when the actors could not keep withstanding the lines they had memorized and shouts erupted. Explosions burst out like inaudible shrieks. The noise was like the shouting voice of a ghost whose living voice had been desecrated. It was this kind of experience of a human voice crying out from outside the door of language's world, asking for a voice, the voice not even dead from being killed. Of the human voice made to suffer the deprivation of language, a voice with the tongue already dead and jumbled with the body. The shrieking cries of the actors sounded also like the voices of some other species arriving at the slaughterhouse. In moments like this, silence is not the opposite of noise but the backside of noise, its figure turned inside out.

Of course, since it was a performance under police supervision, the actors did not utter their lines, instead swallowing and swallowing them into their bodies. It was as if they wanted to be born—a fetus curled up in front of womb door that will not open, calling for the mother outside her body and pounding. And I heard a voice crossing this language without language. It was the sound of a cry mourning for the mother tongue and for this country itself. A voice mourning the excuses of those sitting in the censorship room at City Hall, and at the same time mourning the language of the author who they had deprived of language completely.

Having seen the play's redaction, I cried constantly through the two-hour performance, mumbling in my mouth the corrected lines. The audience, too, cried, without even knowing anything about the play's original contents. The author watched the performance from the lighting booth and looked down at me as I cried. Some time after this, he and I would become family. A few days later, when the director of the intelligence agency shot and killed the president, even theater performances without dialogue ended up banned.

■

The poet writes through their own ghost (death). The poet writes by projecting their being onto the infinity of absence where they do not exist. The projected being, now, is me as the other and me as a (visual) voice. The ghost of a poem was already hiding in the preverbal voice before leading the work of art as it begins, and the ghost of a poem already existed in our voices before we became silent because of this mother tongue. A voice calling for other ghosts (audiences) that wander after disappearing, being discarded, getting hurt, and dying. A voice that is not me but is calling me. A voice that is not you but is calling you. This voice precedes language. It is not subject to linguistics. It does not even have anything to do with communication. Its frequency is so high that it is rather inaudible.

The poet swims forth through the world of language with this ghost's voice. Like the act of imagining the rustling of leaves instead of hearing it, this ghost builds the world of language's inverse with its voice. If there is no ghost created by the poet making themself absent, that work of art has not even a soul. Obscene as it may seem, without the poet's living corpse in the work, there is no living voice of the poet. Conversely, there is no art without the voice that makes the self a ghost. The creation of that ghost, the voice of the self who writes poetry, that is poetry. The poet's ghost reappears in between the poet and the reader. To read a work is to inhale this voice's ghost. The reader loses reading's time, loses their own voice. It is as though the reader comes to be in deullim, the state of being possessed. (The Korean word for this possession by ghosts or other beings, deullim or 들림, is a homonym for verbs of hearing, as well as lifting and stopping by.)

The voice's ethic is not in the ghost's utterance, but in deullim. It is in the translation of deullim. Silence, sighs, and screams, crying out without binding language to the body, to ghosts barely hiding inside language through history's remainder. There are hidden voices like coughs, hiccup noises, and moans. The ghosts crushed to death by history's writing. The ghosts teeming in the voids of history, ghosts hiding inside the words of women. Poets mine ghosts. Dead or alive. That which is life force, Das Ereignis, we cannot hear in the everyday because it is noise—that which does not seem to exist in languages. But that which, when built as a poem, is completely empty in the center of what has been built. The ghost acts through the poem's rhythm. This ghost passing like a transparent mouse through the poet's nostril comes out and encounters the transparent mouse that has come out of the reader's nostril. They breed. Desperately. The poet pretends to record reality and daily life. And pretends to collect and lay out lives. However, through the ghost's voice, the poet is trampling the state of utterance that turns life into language. So poetry, too, is a kind of fiction.

This is not to suggest that poems write out fictional stories, but that the place that springs between the poet and the reader is a kind of fiction. That fictional place is not the place the poet describes in the work. It is a place outside the work, a different place where the ghost's voice meets the reader. This place might be called fiction's home. There lives poetry's ghost, transcending the limits of letters, lives. This ghost functions from outside of the poem like reality to the reader. When the ghost's voice touches this poem from the outside, a map is created for the reader, one very different from a world map. In this place, the letters spin into life; the voice that can be heard from these letters is the voice of the poet's ghost called poetry, which does not belong to anyone else. It is the language carried through rhythm.

If you go from writing poetry to prose, it is not easy to return to poetry. This is because in poetry, the relationship between poet and subject is not one-to-one but many-to-many. To go to and return from the one-to-one world with language requiring no explanation entails several spaceships taking off at once. Poetry is different from prose, which is carried out by the same self with one emotion and logic. Poetry instead may be a genre that refuses writing. Or is written by someone who has been removed from writing and from human time. Poetry is the writing of the rejected. Just as a novel is not only fiction, poetry is not just allusion. It is not a genre that plays hide-and-seek with its critics. Poetry is a voice. It is a voice that makes visible and audible something that has not yet been—what cannot be—verbalized. Meaning has evaporated and disappeared from this voice. So it is before concepts are formed, as in people who have not acquired language. Poetry is written to further disconcert the reader with questions: What ever could this poem mean? What is your ideology? What is your identity?

In poetry, the poetic language does not refer to any object's properties. Because an object cannot be told in one language. Objects, like poets, speak through echoes. The voice created in the encounter between echoes is the language of poetry. The poet's body as a body expanded by objects transplanted into it. But poetry believes that one person's cognitive ability cannot wholly figure a single object. Put your ear to an object. Like polyphonic music, the object emits several layers of voices. In this way, poetry is a kind of silent conversation and a kind of noise of many people muttering, mumbling, and shaking. In which case the poet cannot bear any "voice" other than the divisive, irrational, and affective-reactive voice. In particular, the poetry of women, which has been expelled and killed many worlds over, is not an autonomous subject, but a substance with a body, an amalgam of various organs. I used to think that it was a collection of various organs hanging like one's own body and the voice of all those organs' ghosts mumbling.

The reader of this kind of poetry moves out of their own ego and enters the void of meaning, a sentence with a hole pierced through it. Into the void of words, like Glenn Gould's muttering while playing the piano. Just as objects and life become alternate editions of the original as soon as they are turned into poetic images. The voices of these people are audible every moment of every day. The language that refers to it is language, but it also becomes a cracked voice inside and outside of language. It becomes a drumstick that hits a firm center through its absence.

▪

The most common questions I am asked after poetry readings in Korea are "Why do you write poetry?" and "What do these poems mean?" Korean audiences express directly a kind of frustration after hearing my poems. When I read in other countries, however, there is one question I am always asked: "Why is there surrealism in your poetry?" Following that, those who want to show off their knowledge of Korean literature then specify, "I know that your country was late to engage with surrealism compared to Japan and China. Under whose influence are you writing surrealist poetry?"

Every time I get asked this question, I think: Why do these people label anything unfamiliar as surrealist? In visual art, there are installations, multimedia works, and various expressions, mediums, and methods, but not all of it is called surrealism. In poetry, why do readers use themselves as a standard and call everything they cannot understand surrealism? When expressions, mediums, and methods—or the territory in which a poem is uttered—can otherwise be different. Why does that root *sur*, which came into existence a hundred years ago, still have a sour taste? (The French word *sur* having a tart meaning.) There was no teacher I had who taught me poetry, not even an older poet, no poets who mentored me—yet these people from other countries seem to hope to teach me that surrealism exists. And then I suspect that they flatter themselves by attaching the term "surreal" to what is unfamiliar, anything not written in everyday speech they find easy to read.

I once read a scene in the book *Dada of Gyeongseong, Dada of Tokyo* by Nagi Yoshikawa, in which Ko Han Yong welcomed Japanese Dadaist Jun Tsuji to Gyeongseong (Seoul's name at the time) in 1924 by holding up a flag with "Dadaism" written on it. I laughed very loudly thinking of this scene at Seoul Station on some day a hundred years ago. Might there have been anyone among the crowd saying their hellos and farewells who understood what Dadaism was? Had I been influenced, too, by a surrealist foreigner, perhaps I would go and stand at Incheon International Airport holding a flag with the word "surrealism" written on it.

I answer the recurring question this way: No literature is life itself. Literature is inherently morbid, poetic, sour, and surreal (the word 시, shi, meaning both poetry and sour taste). And even when the word "surrealism" did not exist, surrealism already existed in Korea. It was already being written in supernatural stories and fairy tales under labels like the sinseon story or yuseonsa. It was just that you all gave that name to this literary trend. So my poetry is here and now and since I cannot leave my poetry in this literary place, I build my own place that disappears the grammatical person of first or third, disappears time's domains. I raise the voice of a ghost there. Heo Nanseolheon's poetry provides an example:

After a thousand years living as a widow
she had a destined connection to a person from sky water
The sound of night music from the air makes the moon hanging on the roof's edge ring
The goddess who lived in the northern palace comes down onto her feet

Her eighty-seven-part *Yuseonsa* is *already* the voice of the surreal. It is a kind of self-hypnosis. The word at hand is *no*. It means mourning the here in advance. A woman whose husband is still alive has been widowed. The sixteenth-century poet sat in a dark alcove writing poetry with a garland on her head and an open incense box on her desk. Should I, too, wear a garland on my head, light incense, and write a poem? A figure of the woman poet who had no territory where her poetry could live, she sent herself to the middle space between sky and reality and died at the age of twenty-seven. In reality, the poet was a hostage to patriarchy and to the sorrow of losing all her sons and daughters, but in the world of her poetry, she was a lonely mountain spirit who sought freedom and kept her voice alive in that middle space.

Heo Nanseolheon wrote that she had three regrets: being born in this country, being born a woman, and getting married. How can my three sorrows living in the twenty-first century be so similar? A sixteenth-century woman who experiences her sadness, loneliness, abandonment, and hardship all at once soars from her room every single day. And she stays not in this land, but goes to the moon world. She can't find a place to live in reality so she arranges a new place there. "This country, woman, wife" traverses with her whole body this place that is "not." As she goes, she fills her already dead body with ghosts' voices. These murmuring voices of a corpse that cannot be shared with others. We listen to these voices with our eyes. We listen with our bodies. They reject the territory imposed by paternalistic others and ardently resist the other voice, the voice of norms.

A twenty-seven-year-old woman with no illness took a bath, changed her clothes, and said, "This year is equivalent to 3 by 9. Today the lotus flower got hit with frost and turned red." Heo closed her eyes and never awoke again, leaving a will that said to burn all her writings. Although her in-laws set a roomful of poetry on fire, the works that were passed on to her younger brother Heo Gyun survived and were published in China. A few years later, the progressive Korean scholar and novelist Park Jiwon seemingly responded to the Chinese praise for Heo Nanseolheon's poetry by saying, "In general, it is not inherently beautiful for a woman to recite a poem," while another progressive scholar Hong Dae Yong said, "Though this woman's poetry is of a high level, her virtue was far inferior to her poetry." Although the great male sixteenth-century writers praised freedom, as soon as a woman had a little freedom they rushed to kill her. Tsk tsk. The woman's madness or symptoms may be some "other" state that allows the emergence of a new voice. When this mad, out-of-reality voice takes on a body, it becomes the surrealism of a sixteenth-century female poet.

Heo Nanseolheon wrote poetry in Chinese characters. Perhaps her mother tongue of Hangul, forced on and used by women, was paradoxically an entrenched system that oppressed her and enforced her moral principles. The same-sexed moonland of that woman, one she holds out against the superego called motherland and mother tongue. And the pleasure there, the discovery of this voice that battles with the superego, is Heo Nanseolheon's poetry. The voice screams that this person here is "not," that it is not right to live like this, that this is not the real world.

▪

There were days when everyone in the country seemed mired in absurdity. There were days weeping people poured out of sorrow's castle and swept through the streets like wind. Every day was cloudy, day after day. There were days when I was put under the glaring light of censorship even in my dreams. I was a humble low-level editorial member of the staff at a publishing company — colorless, odorless, anonymous. Who no one would notice even if someone slapped my cheek. Why did the weather seem cloudy every day? I cried in my blanket.

Aside from my editorial work, I was submitting poems I wrote in secret to literary magazines. During that time, a detective called me into the police station and slapped me seven times, demanding I give him the address of the translator of a book published by my publisher. Who gave him the right to spew vulgarities at me? I pick up the room in which I was slapped, as though with tweezers. His office bright like the room I used to bring books to, to be censored. That room where no one had a care even as I was slapped. I can turn off the lights so everywhere is pitch dark but that room, my breath is held on everything but that room, often the only bright room whose image comes up for me.

In that room, a large balding man in a white dress shirt slapped my cheek with his thick hand against my long hair. When I stepped back, he reached out and grabbed my blouse, pulling it and hitting me again. He responded to my "I don't know" by saying, "Are you fucking with me? Are you fucking with me?" and shouting vulgarities. I kept picking myself up with tweezers from that office box, which became smaller than a matchbox. Then I swallowed myself. Still, a muttering voice continued to leak from my throat. A few days later I was absent from work at the publisher and instead wrote one poem at a time through a voice that could barely be heard. I wrote seven in total, one poem for each slap. Because I was scared, it was only some years later I published them, in an edition of *The Hell of That Star*, though I did not include the one that was entirely profanities. That detective was in charge of the publishing company I worked for, and after that he would often show up as though nothing had happened to joke and chat with the editor-in-chief. On those days when he showed up, I would go to the bathroom and stay there for a long time.

People in a story are in the land of that story. If I pull out a story from the human land, the string is so long that even after I wrapped it closed all around my body, there would still be too much left over. Testimonies keep calling back to endless testimonies. With tweezers I pulled out myself, the red string wrapped and wound around my body, then closed the box carrying the man and me and stepped on it. So I threw out the stories of my days at the publishing company. Leaving only the voice behind.

■

The voice that crosses poetry comes to explain that our world, what we believe to be reality, this place that we mistakenly believe exists, is a world of shadows; it comes to inhabit the cracks. The voice of poetry does not believe there is some other place outside this one, but that if you crack this place, you can see a world of absence. That there is another world *in between* for us, that the gap itself exists between us. So, it comes screaming at us that we must break up these images of reality.

The voice of poetry likewise tells us that within each word there is a big void. The space inside is as loud as a chorus. There is certainly no clear subject of the rumblings and vibrations of this chorus. The voice of poetry has no master. I write poetry toward nothingness that has neither master nor subject. The voice of poetry is not a part of language. Not even a part of the body. This voice has no name. It is not dialectical. The voice is not spoken but heard, and only by those who listen. Just an echo. A beat. It is rhythm itself. The voice of poetry is not a plot. It is not about fleshing out some episode.

While living as fragments on the periphery—in the music, in the feelings, in the emotions, without a place to arrive to—it suddenly finds a sound. The figure that is revealed is not an image or an episode, but a voice not wrapped in language. A certain voice is heard along the path where the slain tongue heads toward lost things, or at the border where the tongue is banished and exiled. A poet is a poet only when they hear this voice. A poet is a poet only when they hear the voids between, in words between the writer and the listener.

Korean people often ask me, as a poet, "Why is it you write poetry?" and "What does your poetry mean?" I answer that I cannot possibly live here. I cannot keep living here without dying. I answer that my voice, which has become a ghost, has built a ghost being continuously formed. That poetry is death and the voice of death is plural. When you ask me in other places why I am a surrealist, I answer pleading to please not call me a surrealist. Then I answer that most Korean poetry of a certain age and gender should be called surrealist too, and that the haunted house of my poetry is an empty house where only the voice lives.

In that hole-like house, my poetry is *poetrying*. And through poetry, I am doing *with you*. I answer that I am hitting that wholly empty place with a large drumstick like Princess Nakrang, who abandoned her country for a prince from another by tearing apart the drum that warned of invasions; I am trying to offer a feminine balm instead of the betrayal of dethroning my father, the king. I answer that my voice vibrates the air and spreads the echo and that the wind cries. I answer that the carrying out of my voice as a woman poet takes place within the voids of my mother tongue. That it is only when these feminine and poetic desires are carried out within those voids of my mother tongue that I can finally unfold out a poem.

Notes

"The Guy Who Went Alone" lists two provinces: Gyeongsang-do, where the author was born, and Jeolla-do, whose capital Gwangju was site of the uprising that began on May 18, 1980. Hong Gildong is the protagonist of a Joseon Dynasty-era novel, a character known as a righteous thief; the name has come to generically represent names or characters in general.

"The History of Feed" has a subheading that refers to the line "We who have a four-thousand-year history of eating people" from Lu Xun's *The Diary of a Mad Man*.

"A Sunday of Only Afternoon" is a title that comes from a 1985 song title by the Korean band 들국화 (or deulgukhwa, meaning wild chrysanthemum). The song's chorus goes: "I entered darkness, and walked endlessly, I entered rain, and just kept walking."

"Midstness": "The Errant Translator" was Sawako Nakayasu's November 2023 keynote address at the American Literary Translators Association Conference, hosted with the University of Arizona Poetry Center.

"Poetry Voice": The Korean translation of the Japanese work mentioned here was published as *Dada of Gyeongseong, Dada in Tokyo*, but the original was titled *Dada of Keijō, Dada of Tokyo*. During and after Japanese occupation, Keijō was the colonial capital and the Japanese name for present day Seoul.

The author's selections of Heo Nanseolheon, Park Ji-won, and Hong Dae-yong appear in the translator's translation. The poem quoted is from the thirty-seventh section of eighty-seven.

Hangul is the current Korean alphabet established in the fifteenth century, when the male and elite written language was classical Chinese. The paradox is that the designated women's language was the one in which she was oppressed.

The red string is an East Asian symbol for fate connecting people and circumstance with long invisible threads.

Acknowledgments

Thank you first to Kim Hyesoon 선생님, whose poems bewildered, calmed, disputed, and accompanied me over seven years, and whose book I love in every language.

My thanks to the board and editor of Wesleyan University Press, who made for these poems a gracious and rigorous home, and to Lee Bae, whose charcoal covers it.

Bows and gratitude to dream writer-translators Fady Joudah, Suji Kwock Kim, and Sandra Lim for the models you set for this work and for your words on this collection, sweet shade as it meets sunlight, eyes fluttering.

I am grateful for the mind of Kim Seongeun, who labored over several rounds of drafts with me and entertained their most playful ideas in essential and generative encounters.

Thank you to the writers and translators who specifically encouraged and included me as a translator, including Jeehyun Choi, Sawako Nakayasu, Srikanth Reddy, Jack Jung, Jenna Tang, Kathleen Maris Paltrineri, Robert Wood Lynn, Wendy Chen, Arash Saedinia, and Aron Aji.

Much gratitude to friends, colleagues, and teachers who supported me toward the circumstances that bore this book: Nica Giromini, Mark Levine, Yoon Sun Lee, Jac Jemc, Josh Kalla, Jennifer Galvão, Jane Mah Hutton, Carlos Rafael Gomez, CM Burroughs, Ally Kalt, Leon Pan, Martín Espada, Vanessa Gubbins, Alex Marzano-Lesnevich, Dana Isokawa, Emma Sokoloff, Andrew Leong, Zahra Safaverdi, Desiree C. Bailey, Azadeh Tajpour, Eduardo C. Corral, Terrence Chin-Loy, Monica Youn, Rae Armantrout, and Donika Kelly.

For cherished time and space with grants, thank you to the Helen Dunmore Scholarship at the Banff Centre, Wellesley College, the University of Iowa, the Literature Translation Institute of Korea, Kenyon College, the James Merrill House, and the University of California.

Beaming thanks to the editors and staffs of the journals where poems from this manuscript appeared: *The Massachusetts Review*, *AGNI*, *Gulf Coast*, *Colorado Review*, *The Paris Review*, *Copper Nickel*, *The Hopkins Review*, *Modern Poetry in Translation*, *Bennington Review*, *swamp pink*, *Four Way Review*, *Poet Lore*, *Tupelo Quarterly*, *The Margins*, *Poetry Daily*, *The Cortland Review*, *Hayden Ferry's Review*, *Quarterly West*, *Asymptote*, and *The Nashville Review*. Poems were also graciously chosen as the winner of the 2024 Gulf Coast Prize in Translation and as Editors' Choice for the 2022 and 2023 Anne Frydman Translation Prize. And thank you for the chance to write about the poems' translation in *The Paris Review Daily*, *Copper Nickel*, *Modern Poetry in Translation*, *Poetry Daily*, and *Asymptote*.

I was lucky to be welcomed by organizers at reading series at Open Books, Silo City Reading Series, *The Sewanee Review*, Poetry at Bennington, Auburn's Third Thursday Poetry Series, Desert Nights, Rising Stars Writers Conference, Blacksmith House Poetry Series, Randolph College, Asian American Writers' Workshop, Poetry Society of America, and Brooklyn Poets.

My love to the dear writers who hosted me on their campuses where I connected my work to readers and thinkers and to myself. Airea D. Matthews, Carolina Ebeid, Natanya Pulley, Allison Adelle Hedge Coke, Saddiq Dzukogi, A. Van Jordan, Felicia Zamora, Diana Khoi Nguyen, Susan Nguyen, and Anna Maria Hong: I am thankful for these generous invitations and for your students, who welcomed me and made my words new.

Thank you always to my family, including Willa and Penny, and especially to my mom and all the motherings and ghosts that made me, and my partner with whom I am in every midst, by my favorite providence.

About the Author and Translator

Kim Hyesoon has published fourteen poetry collections in Korean, which have been translated into several languages. A recipient of the Kim Suyeong and Midang awards in South Korea, she has more recently won the Ho-Am Prize in the Arts, the Griffin Poetry Prize, and the Cikada Prize. Kim lives in Seoul and taught creative writing at the Seoul Institute of the Arts for many years.

Cindy Juyoung Ok is the author of *Ward Toward*, which won the Yale Younger Poets Prize and was a finalist for the *Los Angeles Times* Book Prize and the National Book Critics Circle's John Leonard Prize. A former high school physics teacher, Ok is an assistant professor of English.